D0903327

428.1
JoR
2012

Education Resource Center
University of Delaware
Newark, DE 19716-2940

BOOKWORMS

OPPOSITES

Empty Full

Apple Jordan

Marshall Cavendish
Benchmark
New York

T60825

My bowl is empty.

My bowl is full.

My wagon is empty.

My wagon is full.

My bottle is empty.

My bottle is full.

My cart is empty.

My cart is full.

My basket is empty.

My basket is full.

Words We Know

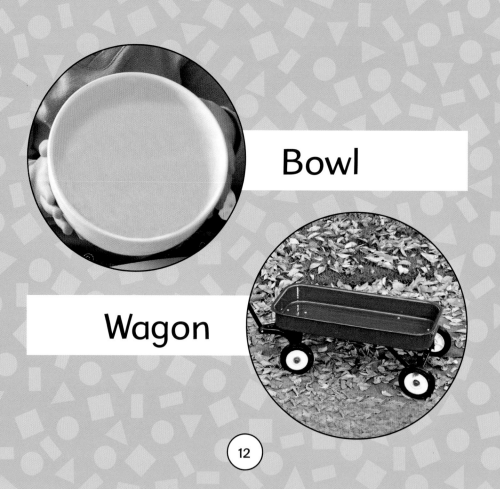

Bowl

Wagon

Bottle

Cart

Basket

Index

Page numbers in **boldface** are illustrations.

About the Author

Apple Jordan has written many books for children, including a number of titles in the Bookworms series. She lives in upstate New York with her husband and two children.

With thanks to the Reading Consultants:

Nanci Vargas, Ed.D., is an Assistant Professor of Elementary Education at the University of Indianapolis.

Beth Walker Gambro is an Adjunct Professor at the University of St. Francis in Joliet, Illinois.

Copyright © 2012 Marshall Cavendish Corporation

Published by Marshall Cavendish Benchmark
An imprint of Marshall Cavendish Corporation

All rights reserved. No part of this publication may be reproduced, stored in a retrieval system or transmitted, in any form or by any means, electronic, mechanical, photocopying, recording, or otherwise, without the prior permission of the copyright owner. Request for permission should be addressed to the Publisher, Marshall Cavendish Corporation, 99 White Plains Road, Tarrytown, NY 10591. Tel: (914) 332-8888, fax: (914) 332-1888. Website: www.marshallcavendish.us

This publication represents the opinions and views of the author based on Apple Jordan's personal experience, knowledge, and research. The information in this book serves as a general guide only. The author and publisher have used their best efforts in preparing this book and disclaim liability rising directly and indirectly from the use and application of this book.

Other Marshall Cavendish Offices:
Marshall Cavendish International (Asia) Private Limited, 1 New Industrial Road, Singapore 536196 • Marshall Cavendish International (Thailand) Co Ltd. 253 Asoke, 12th Flr, Sukhumvit 21 Road, Klongtoey Nua, Wattana, Bangkok 10110, Thailand • Marshall Cavendish (Malaysia) Sdn Bhd, Times Subang, Lot 46, Subang Hi-Tech Industrial Park, Batu Tiga, 40000 Shah Alam, Selangor Darul Ehsan, Malaysia

Marshall Cavendish is a trademark of Times Publishing Limited

Library of Congress
Cataloging-in-Publication Data

Jordan, Apple.
Empty full / Apple Jordan.
p. cm. — (Bookworms. Opposites.)
Includes index.
Summary: "Depicts familiar items that are empty and items that are full to demonstrate the concept of empty and full" —Provided by publisher.
ISBN 978-1-60870-420-0
1. English language—Synonyms and antonyms—Juvenile literature. I. Title.
PE1591.J665 2011
428.1—dc22   2010039536

Editor: Joy Bean
Publisher: Michelle Bisson
Art Director: Anahid Hamparian
Series Designer: Virginia Pope

Photo research by Tracey Engel

Cover: Jaimie Duplass/Shutterstock (left), Ilike/Shutterstock (right);
Title page: Yellow Dog Productions/Getty Images (left), Daniel Hurst Photography/Getty Images (right)

The photographs in this book are used by permission and through the courtesy of: *Getty Images*: Domino, 2, 12 (left); Yellow Dog Productions, 10; Daniel Hurst Photography, 11, 13 (bottom); *Alamy*: MBI, 3; CristinaFumi people, 6; *SuperStock*: Blend Images, 4, 5, 12 (right); *Shutterstock*: Elena Blokhina, 7, 13 (top); Nagy-Bagoly Arpad, 9, 13 (middle); *iStockphoto*: tirc83, 8.

Printed in Malaysia (T)
1 3 5 6 4 2